Larry the Hippo

By: Eleni Romanias

Illustrations By: Jeevanand Surya

Larry the hippo was used to his shelf
But it wasn't the life that he saw for himself.

In the big giant store people walked down his aisle,
And every kid's face that he saw made him smile.

But Larry was small and not like the others.
He could barely be seen behind all of his brothers.

Day after day he would hope for the best
But he never was chosen like all of the rest.

Poor Larry remained on his shelf all alone,
Just waiting for someone to come take him home.

Finally one day someone tall spotted Larry.
She wore a red vest and her name tag said, "Mary."

Seeing Larry alone on the shelf made her sad
But she thought that the space right below wasn't bad.

So she moved Larry lower and set him up front.
Now small kids would see him because of her stunt.

The difference in view was exciting to Larry,
Though he had to admit the change was a bit scary.

When the next day began and kids walked down his aisle,
The little ones stopped and stared for a while.

Larry soaked up the spotlight with new found delight
But the excitement he had was soon turned into fright.

The kids started poking and calling him small.
It wasn't a warm fuzzy feeling at all.

His hope had soon dwindled as the day had gone by.
Rejected and hurt, he about wanted to cry.

"I just want a home," Larry said to himself.
And now he was not even on his own shelf.

But little did he know that the store clerk named Mary
Would come back to check on the small hippo Larry.

When Mary had seen him she said, "That won't do."
For even the small hippos need a home too.

Mary scooped up poor Larry and walked him about.
She paid the cashier and then they were out.

Larry couldn't believe this was finally it.
The car ride was long but he didn't mind a bit.

When they walked through the door a young boy was there.
Mary handed him Larry, and he held him with care.

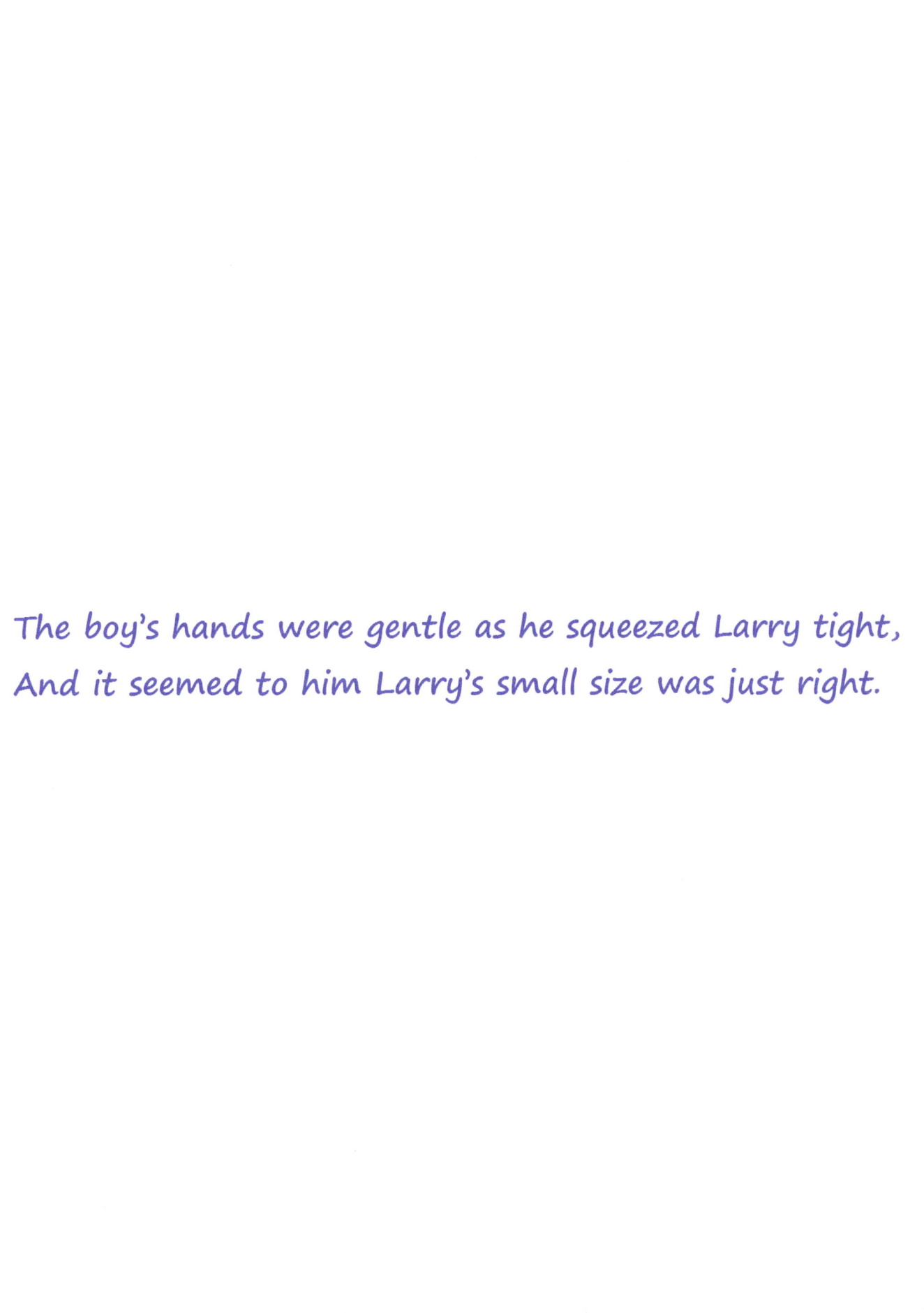

The boy's hands were gentle as he squeezed Larry tight,
And it seemed to him Larry's small size was just right.

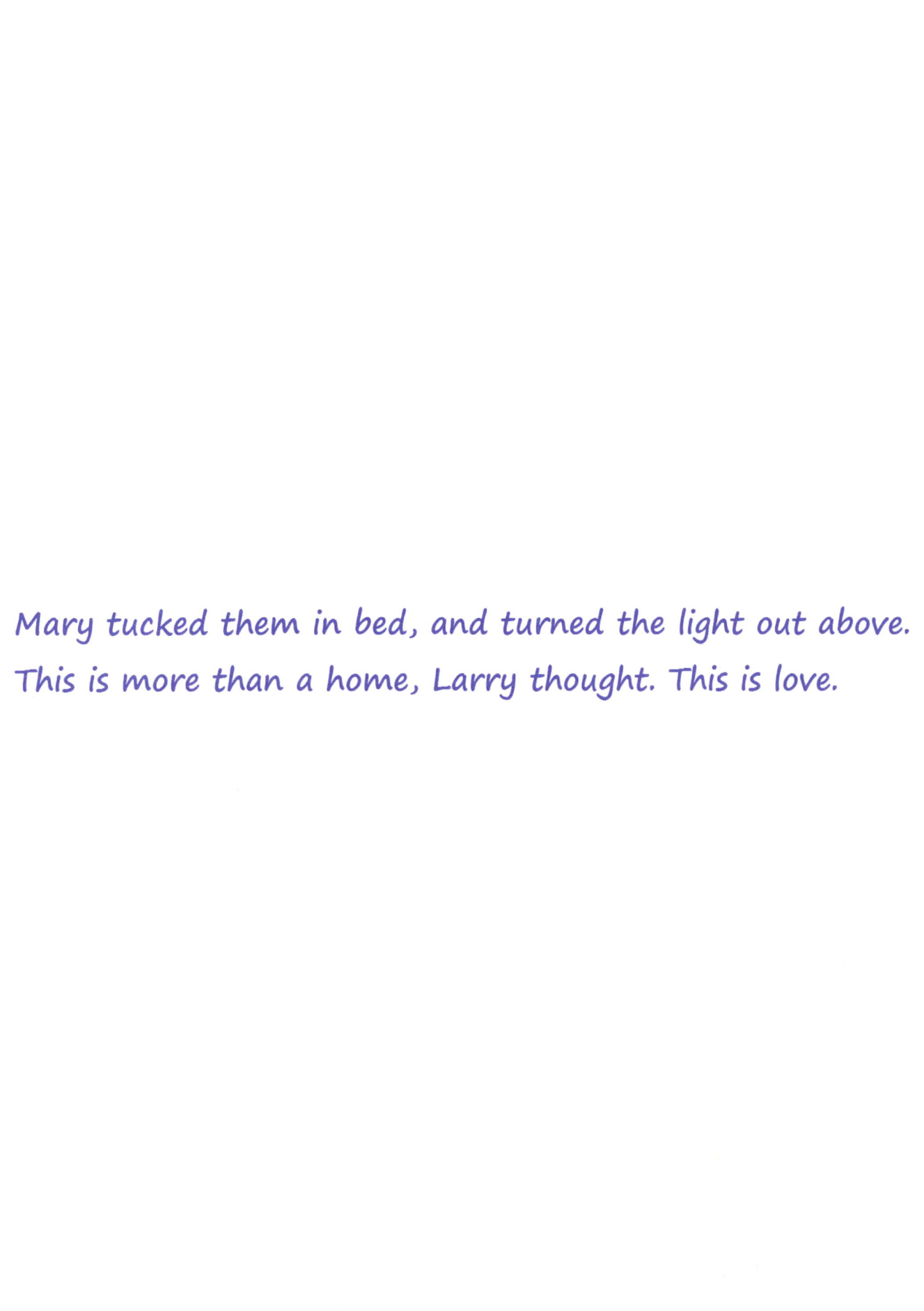

Mary tucked them in bed, and turned the light out above.
This is more than a home, Larry thought. This is love.

THE END

CPSIA information can be obtained
at www.ICGtesting.com
Printed in the USA
BVHW021951250621
610446BV00002B/115